THIS FIELD TRIP PLANNER BELONGS TO:

_____

DEDICATION

This Field Trip Log Book is dedicated to all the Teachers out there who love to plan out their school season field trip activities, and love to document their findings in the process.

You are my inspiration for producing books and I'm honored to be a part of keeping all of your field trip information and records organized.

How to use this Field Trip Log Book:

This useful field trip planner is a must-have for anyone that needs to record their school field trip activities! You will love this easy to use field trip log book to track and record all your school season activities.

Each interior page includes space to record & track the following:

Destination and Date - Record where the field trip destination will be taking place and the date of the activity.
Learning Goal - Use this space to fill in the learning goal of the field trip.
Contact Information - Record the contact information of each student.
Curriculum Points - Fill in the points obtained to fulfill the curriculum requirements.
Packing List - Stay on task by writing down what will be needed for this field trip.
Preparation Study - Record any study required before the field trip is taken.
What Happened/What Did I Learn - Write down in this space what took place on the field trip, and what lessons were learned.
Notes - Extra note space to record any thoughts or observations from the field trip.

If you are new to homeschooling or taking field trips for school, this field trip planning log book is a must have! Can make a great useful gift for anyone that loves to take field trips!

Enjoy!

Field Trip Planner

Destination _____

Date _____

Learning Goal _____

Contacts _____ _____

_____ _____

Curriculum Points	Packing List	Preparation Study
•	•	•
•	•	•
•	•	•
•	•	•
•	•	•

What happened?	What did I learn?

Notes _____

_____

_____

Field Trip Planner

Destination _____

Date _____

Learning Goal _____

Contacts _____ _____

_____ _____

Curriculum Points
-
-
-
-
-

Packing List
-
-
-
-
-

Preparation Study
-
-
-
-
-

What happened?	What did I learn?

Notes _____

_____

_____

Field Trip Planner

Destination _____

Date _____

Learning Goal _____

Contacts _____ _____

_____

Curriculum Points
-
-
-
-
-

Packing List
-
-
-
-
-

Preparation Study
-
-
-
-
-

What happened?	What did I learn?

Notes _____

_____

_____

Field Trip Planner

Destination _____

Date _____

Learning Goal _____

Contacts _____ _____

_____ _____

Curriculum Points
-
-
-
-
-

Packing List
-
-
-
-
-

Preparation Study
-
-
-
-
-

What happened?	What did I learn?

Notes _____

_____

_____

Field Trip Planner

Destination _____

Date _____

Learning Goal _____

Contacts _____ _____

_____

Curriculum Points
-
-
-
-
-

Packing List
-
-
-
-
-

Preparation Study
-
-
-
-
-

What happened?	What did I learn?

Notes _____

_____

_____

Field Trip Planner

Destination _____

Date _____

Learning Goal _____

Contacts _____ _____

_____ _____

Curriculum Points
-
-
-
-
-

Packing List
-
-
-
-
-

Preparation Study
-
-
-
-
-

What happened?	What did I learn?

Notes _____

_____

_____

Field Trip Planner

Destination _____

Date _____

Learning Goal _____

Contacts _____ _____

_____

Curriculum Points
-
-
-
-
-

Packing List
-
-
-
-
-

Preparation Study
-
-
-
-
-

What happened?	What did I learn?

Notes _____

_____

_____

Field Trip Planner

Destination _____

Date _____

Learning Goal _____

Contacts _____   _____

_____   _____

Curriculum Points
-
-
-
-
-

Packing List
-
-
-
-
-

Preparation Study
-
-
-
-
-

What happened?	What did I learn?

Notes _____

_____

Field Trip Planner

Destination _____

Date _____

Learning Goal _____

Contacts _____ _____

_____ _____

Curriculum Points
-
-
-
-
-

Packing List
-
-
-
-
-

Preparation Study
-
-
-
-
-

What happened?	What did I learn?

Notes _____

_____

_____

Field Trip Planner

Destination _____

Date _____

Learning Goal _____

Contacts _____ _____

_____ _____

Curriculum Points
-
-
-
-
-

Packing List
-
-
-
-
-

Preparation Study
-
-
-
-
-

What happened?	What did I learn?

Notes _____

_____

_____

Field Trip Planner

Destination _____

Date _____

Learning Goal _____

Contacts _____ _____

_____ _____

Curriculum Points
-
-
-
-
-

Packing List
-
-
-
-
-

Preparation Study
-
-
-
-
-

What happened?	What did I learn?

Notes _____

_____

_____

Field Trip Planner

Destination _____

Date _____

Learning Goal _____

Contacts _____ _____

_____ _____

Curriculum Points
-
-
-
-
-

Packing List
-
-
-
-
-

Preparation Study
-
-
-
-
-

What happened?	What did I learn?

Notes _____

_____

_____

Field Trip Planner

Destination _____

Date _____

Learning Goal _____

Contacts _____

_____

Curriculum Points	Packing List	Preparation Study
•	•	•
•	•	•
•	•	•
•	•	•
•	•	•

What happened?	What did I learn?

Notes _____

_____

_____

Field Trip Planner

Destination _____

Date _____

Learning Goal _____

Contacts _____ _____

_____ _____

Curriculum Points
-
-
-
-
-

Packing List
-
-
-
-
-

Preparation Study
-
-
-
-
-

What happened?	What did I learn?

Notes _____

_____

_____

Field Trip Planner

Destination _____

Date _____

Learning Goal _____

Contacts _____   _____

_____

Curriculum Points
-
-
-
-
-

Packing List
-
-
-
-
-

Preparation Study
-
-
-
-
-

What happened?	What did I learn?

Notes _____

_____

_____

Field Trip Planner

Destination _____

Date _____

Learning Goal _____

Contacts _____ _____

_____ _____

Curriculum Points
-
-
-
-
-

Packing List
-
-
-
-
-

Preparation Study
-
-
-
-
-

What happened?	What did I learn?

Notes _____

_____

_____

Field Trip Planner

Destination _____

Date _____

Learning Goal _____

Contacts _____ _____

_____ _____

Curriculum Points
-
-
-
-
-

Packing List
-
-
-
-
-

Preparation Study
-
-
-
-
-

What happened?	What did I learn?

Notes _____

_____

_____

Field Trip Planner

Destination _____

Date _____

Learning Goal _____

Contacts _____   _____

_____   _____

Curriculum Points
-
-
-
-
-

Packing List
-
-
-
-
-

Preparation Study
-
-
-
-
-

What happened?	What did I learn?

Notes _____

_____

Field Trip Planner

Destination _____

Date _____

Learning Goal _____

Contacts _____

_____

Curriculum Points
-
-
-
-
-

Packing List
-
-
-
-
-

Preparation Study
-
-
-
-
-

What happened?	What did I learn?

Notes _____

_____

Field Trip Planner

Destination _____

Date _____

Learning Goal _____

Contacts _____ _____

_____ _____

Curriculum Points
-
-
-
-
-

Packing List
-
-
-
-
-

Preparation Study
-
-
-
-
-

What happened?	What did I learn?

Notes _____

_____

_____

Field Trip Planner

Destination _____

Date _____

Learning Goal _____

Contacts _____ _____

_____

Curriculum Points
-
-
-
-
-

Packing List
-
-
-
-
-

Preparation Study
-
-
-
-
-

What happened?	What did I learn?

Notes _____

_____

_____

Field Trip Planner

Destination _____

Date _____

Learning Goal _____

Contacts _____ _____

_____ _____

Curriculum Points
-
-
-
-
-

Packing List
-
-
-
-
-

Preparation Study
-
-
-
-
-

What happened?	What did I learn?

Notes _____

_____

_____

Field Trip Planner

Destination _____

Date _____

Learning Goal _____

Contacts _____ _____

_____ _____

Curriculum Points
-
-
-
-
-

Packing List
-
-
-
-
-

Preparation Study
-
-
-
-
-

What happened?	What did I learn?

Notes _____

_____

_____

Field Trip Planner

Destination _____

Date _____

Learning Goal _____

Contacts _____

Curriculum Points	Packing List	Preparation Study
•	•	•
•	•	•
•	•	•
•	•	•
•	•	•

What happened?	What did I learn?

Notes _____

Field Trip Planner

Destination _____

Date _____

Learning Goal _____

Contacts _____

_____

Curriculum Points
-
-
-
-
-

Packing List
-
-
-
-
-

Preparation Study
-
-
-
-
-

What happened?	What did I learn?

Notes _____

_____

_____

Field Trip Planner

Destination _____

Date _____

Learning Goal _____

Contacts _____ _____

_____ _____

Curriculum Points
-
-
-
-
-

Packing List
-
-
-
-
-

Preparation Study
-
-
-
-
-

What happened?	What did I learn?

Notes _____

_____

_____

Field Trip Planner

Destination _____

Date _____

Learning Goal _____

Contacts _____ _____

_____ _____

Curriculum Points
-
-
-
-
-

Packing List
-
-
-
-
-

Preparation Study
-
-
-
-
-

What happened?	What did I learn?

Notes _____

_____

_____

Field Trip Planner

Destination _____

Date _____

Learning Goal _____

Contacts _____   _____

_____   _____

Curriculum Points
-
-
-
-
-

Packing List
-
-
-
-
-

Preparation Study
-
-
-
-
-

What happened?	What did I learn?

Notes _____

_____

_____

Field Trip Planner

Destination _____

Date _____

Learning Goal _____

Contacts _____ _____

_____

Curriculum Points
-
-
-
-
-

Packing List
-
-
-
-
-

Preparation Study
-
-
-
-
-

What happened?	What did I learn?

Notes _____

_____

_____

Field Trip Planner

Destination _____

Date _____

Learning Goal _____

Contacts _____ _____

_____ _____

Curriculum Points
-
-
-
-
-

Packing List
-
-
-
-
-

Preparation Study
-
-
-
-
-

What happened?	What did I learn?

Notes _____

_____

_____

Field Trip Planner

Destination _____

Date _____

Learning Goal _____

Contacts _____ _____

_____

Curriculum Points
-
-
-
-
-

Packing List
-
-
-
-
-

Preparation Study
-
-
-
-
-

What happened?	What did I learn?

Notes _____

_____

_____

Field Trip Planner

Destination _____

Date _____

Learning Goal _____

Contacts _____ _____

_____ _____

Curriculum Points
-
-
-
-
-

Packing List
-
-
-
-
-

Preparation Study
-
-
-
-
-

What happened?	What did I learn?

Notes _____

_____

_____

Field Trip Planner

Destination _____

Date _____

Learning Goal _____

Contacts _____ _____

_____ _____

Curriculum Points
-
-
-
-
-

Packing List
-
-
-
-
-

Preparation Study
-
-
-
-
-

What happened?	What did I learn?

Notes _____

_____

_____

Field Trip Planner

Destination _____

Date _____

Learning Goal _____

Contacts _____ _____

_____ _____

Curriculum Points
-
-
-
-
-

Packing List
-
-
-
-
-

Preparation Study
-
-
-
-
-

What happened?	What did I learn?

Notes _____

_____

_____

Field Trip Planner

Destination _____

Date _____

Learning Goal _____

Contacts _____ _____

_____

Curriculum Points
-
-
-
-
-

Packing List
-
-
-
-
-

Preparation Study
-
-
-
-
-

What happened?	What did I learn?

Notes _____

_____

_____

Field Trip Planner

Destination _____

Date _____

Learning Goal _____

Contacts _____ _____

_____ _____

Curriculum Points
-
-
-
-
-

Packing List
-
-
-
-
-

Preparation Study
-
-
-
-
-

What happened?	What did I learn?

Notes _____

_____

_____

Field Trip Planner

Destination _____

Date _____

Learning Goal _____

Contacts _____

_____

Curriculum Points
-
-
-
-
-

Packing List
-
-
-
-
-

Preparation Study
-
-
-
-
-

What happened?	What did I learn?

Notes _____

_____

_____

Field Trip Planner

Destination _____

Date _____

Learning Goal _____

Contacts _____ _____

_____ _____

Curriculum Points
-
-
-
-
-

Packing List
-
-
-
-
-

Preparation Study
-
-
-
-
-

What happened?	What did I learn?

Notes _____

_____

_____

Field Trip Planner

Destination _____

Date _____

Learning Goal _____

Contacts _____ _____

Curriculum Points
-
-
-
-
-

Packing List
-
-
-
-
-

Preparation Study
-
-
-
-
-

What happened?	What did I learn?

Notes _____
_____
_____

Field Trip Planner

Destination _____

Date _____

Learning Goal _____

Contacts _____ _____

_____ _____

Curriculum Points
-
-
-
-
-

Packing List
-
-
-
-
-

Preparation Study
-
-
-
-
-

What happened?	What did I learn?

Notes _____

_____

_____

Field Trip Planner

Destination _____

Date _____

Learning Goal _____

Contacts _____ _____

_____ _____

Curriculum Points
-
-
-
-
-

Packing List
-
-
-
-
-

Preparation Study
-
-
-
-
-

What happened?	What did I learn?

Notes _____

_____

_____

Field Trip Planner

Destination _____

Date _____

Learning Goal _____

Contacts _____ _____

_____ _____

Curriculum Points
-
-
-
-
-

Packing List
-
-
-
-
-

Preparation Study
-
-
-
-
-

What happened?	What did I learn?

Notes _____

_____

_____

Field Trip Planner

Destination _____

Date _____

Learning Goal _____

Contacts _____
_____ _____

Curriculum Points
-
-
-
-
-

Packing List
-
-
-
-
-

Preparation Study
-
-
-
-
-

What happened?	What did I learn?

Notes _____
_____
_____

Field Trip Planner

Destination _____

Date _____

Learning Goal _____

Contacts _____ _____

_____ _____

Curriculum Points
-
-
-
-
-

Packing List
-
-
-
-
-

Preparation Study
-
-
-
-
-

What happened?	What did I learn?

Notes _____

_____

_____

Field Trip Planner

Destination _____

Date _____

Learning Goal _____

Contacts _____

_____

Curriculum Points
-
-
-
-
-

Packing List
-
-
-
-
-

Preparation Study
-
-
-
-
-

What happened?	What did I learn?

Notes _____

_____

_____

Field Trip Planner

Destination _____

Date _____

Learning Goal _____

Contacts _____ _____

_____ _____

Curriculum Points
-
-
-
-
-

Packing List
-
-
-
-
-

Preparation Study
-
-
-
-
-

What happened?	What did I learn?

Notes _____

_____

_____

Field Trip Planner

Destination _____

Date _____

Learning Goal _____

Contacts _____ _____

_____

Curriculum Points
-
-
-
-
-

Packing List
-
-
-
-
-

Preparation Study
-
-
-
-
-

What happened?	What did I learn?

Notes _____

_____

_____

Field Trip Planner

Destination _____

Date _____

Learning Goal _____

Contacts _____ _____

_____ _____

Curriculum Points
-
-
-
-
-

Packing List
-
-
-
-
-

Preparation Study
-
-
-
-
-

What happened?	What did I learn?

Notes _____

_____

_____

Field Trip Planner

Destination _____

Date _____

Learning Goal _____

Contacts _____ _____

_____

Curriculum Points
-
-
-
-
-

Packing List
-
-
-
-
-

Preparation Study
-
-
-
-
-

What happened?	What did I learn?

Notes _____

_____

_____

Field Trip Planner

Destination _____

Date _____

Learning Goal _____

Contacts _____ _____
_____ _____

Curriculum Points
-
-
-
-
-

Packing List
-
-
-
-
-

Preparation Study
-
-
-
-
-

What happened?	What did I learn?

Notes _____
_____
_____

Field Trip Planner

Destination _____

Date _____

Learning Goal _____

Contacts _____ _____

_____

Curriculum Points
-
-
-
-
-

Packing List
-
-
-
-
-

Preparation Study
-
-
-
-
-

What happened?	What did I learn?

Notes _____

_____

_____

Field Trip Planner

Destination _____

Date _____

Learning Goal _____

Contacts _____ _____

_____ _____

Curriculum Points
-
-
-
-
-

Packing List
-
-
-
-
-

Preparation Study
-
-
-
-
-

What happened?	What did I learn?

Notes _____

_____

_____

Field Trip Planner

Destination _____

Date _____

Learning Goal _____

Contacts _____
_____

Curriculum Points
-
-
-
-
-

Packing List
-
-
-
-
-

Preparation Study
-
-
-
-
-

What happened?	What did I learn?

Notes _____
_____
_____

Field Trip Planner

Destination _____

Date _____

Learning Goal _____

Contacts _____ _____

_____ _____

Curriculum Points
-
-
-
-
-

Packing List
-
-
-
-
-

Preparation Study
-
-
-
-
-

What happened?	What did I learn?

Notes _____

_____

_____

Field Trip Planner

Destination _____

Date _____

Learning Goal _____

Contacts _____

_____

Curriculum Points
-
-
-
-
-

Packing List
-
-
-
-
-

Preparation Study
-
-
-
-
-

What happened?	What did I learn?

Notes _____

_____

_____

Field Trip Planner

Destination _____

Date _____

Learning Goal _____

Contacts _____ _____

_____ _____

Curriculum Points
-
-
-
-
-

Packing List
-
-
-
-
-

Preparation Study
-
-
-
-
-

What happened?	What did I learn?

Notes _____

_____

_____

Field Trip Planner

Destination _____

Date _____

Learning Goal _____

Contacts _____ _____

_____ _____

Curriculum Points
-
-
-
-
-

Packing List
-
-
-
-
-

Preparation Study
-
-
-
-
-

What happened?	What did I learn?

Notes _____

_____

_____

Field Trip Planner

Destination _____

Date _____

Learning Goal _____

Contacts _____ _____

_____ _____

Curriculum Points
-
-
-
-
-

Packing List
-
-
-
-
-

Preparation Study
-
-
-
-
-

What happened?	What did I learn?

Notes _____

_____

_____

Field Trip Planner

Destination _____

Date _____

Learning Goal _____

Contacts _____ _____

_____

Curriculum Points
-
-
-
-
-

Packing List
-
-
-
-
-

Preparation Study
-
-
-
-
-

What happened?	What did I learn?

Notes _____

_____

_____

Field Trip Planner

Destination _____

Date _____

Learning Goal _____

Contacts _____ _____

_____ _____

Curriculum Points
-
-
-
-
-

Packing List
-
-
-
-
-

Preparation Study
-
-
-
-
-

What happened?	What did I learn?

Notes _____

_____

_____

Field Trip Planner

Destination _____

Date _____

Learning Goal _____

Contacts _____ _____

_____ _____

Curriculum Points
-
-
-
-
-

Packing List
-
-
-
-
-

Preparation Study
-
-
-
-
-

What happened?	What did I learn?

Notes _____

_____

_____

Field Trip Planner

Destination _____

Date _____

Learning Goal _____

Contacts _____ _____

_____

Curriculum Points
-
-
-
-
-

Packing List
-
-
-
-
-

Preparation Study
-
-
-
-
-

What happened?	What did I learn?

Notes _____

_____

_____

Field Trip Planner

Destination _____

Date _____

Learning Goal _____

Contacts _____ _____

_____ _____

Curriculum Points
-
-
-
-
-

Packing List
-
-
-
-
-

Preparation Study
-
-
-
-
-

What happened?	What did I learn?

Notes _____

_____

_____

Field Trip Planner

Destination _____

Date _____

Learning Goal _____

Contacts _____ _____

_____ _____

Curriculum Points
-
-
-
-
-

Packing List
-
-
-
-
-

Preparation Study
-
-
-
-
-

What happened?	What did I learn?

Notes _____

_____

_____

Field Trip Planner

Destination _____

Date _____

Learning Goal _____

Contacts _____ _____

_____

Curriculum Points
-
-
-
-
-

Packing List
-
-
-
-
-

Preparation Study
-
-
-
-
-

What happened?	What did I learn?

Notes _____

_____

_____

Field Trip Planner

Destination _____

Date _____

Learning Goal _____

Contacts _____ _____

_____ _____

Curriculum Points
-
-
-
-
-

Packing List
-
-
-
-
-

Preparation Study
-
-
-
-
-

What happened?	What did I learn?

Notes _____

_____

_____

Field Trip Planner

Destination _____

Date _____

Learning Goal _____

Contacts _____
_____
_____

Curriculum Points
-
-
-
-
-

Packing List
-
-
-
-
-

Preparation Study
-
-
-
-
-

What happened?	What did I learn?

Notes _____
_____
_____

Field Trip Planner

Destination _____

Date _____

Learning Goal _____

Contacts _____ _____
_____ _____

Curriculum Points
-
-
-
-
-

Packing List
-
-
-
-
-

Preparation Study
-
-
-
-
-

What happened?	What did I learn?

Notes _____
_____
_____

Field Trip Planner

Destination _____

Date _____

Learning Goal _____

Contacts _____ _____

_____ _____

Curriculum Points
-
-
-
-
-

Packing List
-
-
-
-
-

Preparation Study
-
-
-
-
-

What happened?	What did I learn?

Notes _____

_____

_____

Field Trip Planner

Destination _____

Date _____

Learning Goal _____

Contacts _____ _____

_____

Curriculum Points
-
-
-
-
-

Packing List
-
-
-
-
-

Preparation Study
-
-
-
-
-

What happened?	What did I learn?

Notes _____

_____

_____

Field Trip Planner

Destination _____

Date _____

Learning Goal _____

Contacts _____   _____

_____

Curriculum Points
-
-
-
-
-

Packing List
-
-
-
-
-

Preparation Study
-
-
-
-
-

What happened?	What did I learn?

Notes _____

_____

_____

Field Trip Planner

Destination _____

Date _____

Learning Goal _____

Contacts _____
_____

Curriculum Points
-
-
-
-
-

Packing List
-
-
-
-
-

Preparation Study
-
-
-
-
-

What happened?	What did I learn?

Notes _____
_____
_____

Field Trip Planner

Destination _____

Date _____

Learning Goal _____

Contacts _____ _____

_____

Curriculum Points
-
-
-
-
-

Packing List
-
-
-
-
-

Preparation Study
-
-
-
-
-

What happened?	What did I learn?

Notes _____

_____

_____

Field Trip Planner

Destination _____

Date _____

Learning Goal _____

Contacts _____ _____

_____ _____

Curriculum Points
-
-
-
-
-

Packing List
-
-
-
-
-

Preparation Study
-
-
-
-
-

What happened?	What did I learn?

Notes _____

_____

Field Trip Planner

Destination _____

Date _____

Learning Goal _____

Contacts _____ _____

_____

Curriculum Points
-
-
-
-
-

Packing List
-
-
-
-
-

Preparation Study
-
-
-
-
-

What happened?	What did I learn?

Notes _____

_____

_____

Field Trip Planner

Destination _____

Date _____

Learning Goal _____

Contacts _____ _____

_____ _____

Curriculum Points
-
-
-
-
-

Packing List
-
-
-
-
-

Preparation Study
-
-
-
-
-

What happened?	What did I learn?

Notes _____

_____

_____

Field Trip Planner

Destination _____

Date _____

Learning Goal _____

Contacts _____   _____

_____

Curriculum Points
-
-
-
-
-

Packing List
-
-
-
-
-

Preparation Study
-
-
-
-
-

What happened?	What did I learn?

Notes _____

_____

_____

Field Trip Planner

Destination _____

Date _____

Learning Goal _____

Contacts _____ _____

_____ _____

Curriculum Points
-
-
-
-
-

Packing List
-
-
-
-
-

Preparation Study
-
-
-
-
-

What happened?	What did I learn?

Notes _____

_____

_____

Field Trip Planner

Destination _____

Date _____

Learning Goal _____

Contacts _____ _____

_____

Curriculum Points
-
-
-
-
-

Packing List
-
-
-
-
-

Preparation Study
-
-
-
-
-

What happened?	What did I learn?

Notes _____

_____

_____

Field Trip Planner

Destination _____

Date _____

Learning Goal _____

Contacts _____ _____

_____ _____

Curriculum Points
-
-
-
-
-

Packing List
-
-
-
-
-

Preparation Study
-
-
-
-
-

What happened?	What did I learn?

Notes _____

_____

_____

Field Trip Planner

Destination _____

Date _____

Learning Goal _____

Contacts _____ _____

_____

Curriculum Points
-
-
-
-
-

Packing List
-
-
-
-
-

Preparation Study
-
-
-
-
-

What happened?	What did I learn?

Notes _____

_____

_____

Field Trip Planner

Destination _____

Date _____

Learning Goal _____

Contacts _____ _____

_____ _____

Curriculum Points
-
-
-
-
-

Packing List
-
-
-
-
-

Preparation Study
-
-
-
-
-

What happened?	What did I learn?

Notes _____

_____

_____

Field Trip Planner

Destination _____

Date _____

Learning Goal _____

Contacts _____ _____

_____ _____

Curriculum Points
-
-
-
-
-

Packing List
-
-
-
-
-

Preparation Study
-
-
-
-
-

What happened?	What did I learn?

Notes _____

_____

_____

Field Trip Planner

Destination _____

Date _____

Learning Goal _____

Contacts _____ _____

_____ _____

Curriculum Points
-
-
-
-
-

Packing List
-
-
-
-
-

Preparation Study
-
-
-
-
-

What happened?	What did I learn?

Notes _____

_____

_____

Field Trip Planner

Destination _____

Date _____

Learning Goal _____

Contacts _____ _____

_____

Curriculum Points
-
-
-
-
-

Packing List
-
-
-
-
-

Preparation Study
-
-
-
-
-

What happened?	What did I learn?

Notes _____

_____

_____

Field Trip Planner

Destination _____

Date _____

Learning Goal _____

Contacts _____ _____

_____ _____

Curriculum Points
-
-
-
-
-

Packing List
-
-
-
-
-

Preparation Study
-
-
-
-
-

What happened?	What did I learn?

Notes _____

_____

_____

Field Trip Planner

Destination _____

Date _____

Learning Goal _____

Contacts _____ _____

_____ _____

Curriculum Points
-
-
-
-
-

Packing List
-
-
-
-
-

Preparation Study
-
-
-
-
-

What happened?	What did I learn?

Notes _____

_____

_____

Field Trip Planner

Destination _____

Date _____

Learning Goal _____

Contacts _____ _____

_____ _____

Curriculum Points
-
-
-
-
-

Packing List
-
-
-
-
-

Preparation Study
-
-
-
-
-

What happened?	What did I learn?

Notes _____

_____

_____

Field Trip Planner

Destination _____

Date _____

Learning Goal _____

Contacts _____ _____

_____

Curriculum Points
-
-
-
-
-

Packing List
-
-
-
-
-

Preparation Study
-
-
-
-
-

What happened?	What did I learn?

Notes _____

_____

_____

Field Trip Planner

Destination _____

Date _____

Learning Goal _____

Contacts _____ _____

_____

Curriculum Points
-
-
-
-
-

Packing List
-
-
-
-
-

Preparation Study
-
-
-
-
-

What happened?	What did I learn?

Notes _____

_____

_____

Field Trip Planner

Destination _____

Date _____

Learning Goal _____

Contacts _____   _____

_____   _____

Curriculum Points
-
-
-
-
-

Packing List
-
-
-
-
-

Preparation Study
-
-
-
-
-

What happened?	What did I learn?

Notes _____

_____

_____

Field Trip Planner

Destination _____

Date _____

Learning Goal _____

Contacts _____ _____

_____ _____

Curriculum Points
-
-
-
-
-

Packing List
-
-
-
-
-

Preparation Study
-
-
-
-
-

What happened?	What did I learn?

Notes _____

_____

_____

Field Trip Planner

Destination _____

Date _____

Learning Goal _____

Contacts _____

_____

Curriculum Points	Packing List	Preparation Study
•	•	•
•	•	•
•	•	•
•	•	•
•	•	•

What happened?	What did I learn?

Notes _____

_____

_____

Field Trip Planner

Destination _____

Date _____

Learning Goal _____

Contacts _____ _____

_____ _____

Curriculum Points
-
-
-
-
-

Packing List
-
-
-
-
-

Preparation Study
-
-
-
-
-

What happened?	What did I learn?

Notes _____

_____

_____

Field Trip Planner

Destination _____

Date _____

Learning Goal _____

Contacts _____ _____

_____ _____

Curriculum Points
-
-
-
-
-

Packing List
-
-
-
-
-

Preparation Study
-
-
-
-
-

What happened?	What did I learn?

Notes _____

_____

_____

Field Trip Planner

Destination _____

Date _____

Learning Goal _____

Contacts _____ _____

_____ _____

Curriculum Points
-
-
-
-
-

Packing List
-
-
-
-
-

Preparation Study
-
-
-
-
-

What happened?	What did I learn?

Notes _____

_____

_____

Field Trip Planner

Destination _____

Date _____

Learning Goal _____

Contacts _____ _____

_____

Curriculum Points
-
-
-
-
-

Packing List
-
-
-
-
-

Preparation Study
-
-
-
-
-

What happened?	What did I learn?

Notes _____

_____

_____

Field Trip Planner

Destination _____

Date _____

Learning Goal _____

Contacts _____

Curriculum Points
-
-
-
-
-

Packing List
-
-
-
-
-

Preparation Study
-
-
-
-
-

What happened?	What did I learn?

Notes _____

Field Trip Planner

Destination _____

Date _____

Learning Goal _____

Contacts _____ _____

_____

Curriculum Points
-
-
-
-
-

Packing List
-
-
-
-
-

Preparation Study
-
-
-
-
-

What happened?	What did I learn?

Notes _____

_____

Field Trip Planner

Destination _____

Date _____

Learning Goal _____

Contacts _____ _____

_____ _____

Curriculum Points	Packing List	Preparation Study
•	•	•
•	•	•
•	•	•
•	•	•
•	•	•

What happened?	What did I learn?

Notes _____

_____

_____

Field Trip Planner

Destination _____

Date _____

Learning Goal _____

Contacts _____ _____

_____ _____

Curriculum Points
-
-
-
-
-

Packing List
-
-
-
-
-

Preparation Study
-
-
-
-
-

What happened?	What did I learn?

Notes _____

_____

_____

Field Trip Planner

Destination _____

Date _____

Learning Goal _____

Contacts _____   _____

_____

Curriculum Points
-
-
-
-
-

Packing List
-
-
-
-
-

Preparation Study
-
-
-
-
-

What happened?	What did I learn?

Notes _____

_____

_____

Field Trip Planner

Destination _____

Date _____

Learning Goal _____

Contacts _____ _____

_____

Curriculum Points
-
-
-
-
-

Packing List
-
-
-
-
-

Preparation Study
-
-
-
-
-

What happened?	What did I learn?

Notes _____

_____

_____

Field Trip Planner

Destination _____

Date _____

Learning Goal _____

Contacts _____ _____

_____ _____

Curriculum Points
-
-
-
-
-

Packing List
-
-
-
-
-

Preparation Study
-
-
-
-
-

What happened?	What did I learn?

Notes _____

_____

_____

Field Trip Planner

Destination _____

Date _____

Learning Goal _____

Contacts _____

Curriculum Points
-
-
-
-
-

Packing List
-
-
-
-
-

Preparation Study
-
-
-
-
-

What happened?	What did I learn?

Notes _____

Field Trip Planner

Destination _____

Date _____

Learning Goal _____

Contacts _____ _____

_____ _____

Curriculum Points
-
-
-
-
-

Packing List
-
-
-
-
-

Preparation Study
-
-
-
-
-

What happened?	What did I learn?

Notes _____

_____

_____

Field Trip Planner

Destination _____

Date _____

Learning Goal _____

Contacts _____ _____

_____

Curriculum Points
-
-
-
-
-

Packing List
-
-
-
-
-

Preparation Study
-
-
-
-
-

What happened?	What did I learn?

Notes _____

_____

_____

www.ingramcontent.com/pod-product-compliance
Lightning Source LLC
Chambersburg PA
CBHW081155070526
44583CB00021B/2854